The Rain Barrel
Nicholas McLachlan

salmonpoetry

Published in 2015 by
Salmon Poetry
Cliffs of Moher, County Clare, Ireland
Website: www.salmonpoetry.com
Email: info@salmonpoetry.com

Copyright © Nicholas McLachlan, 2015

ISBN 978-1-910669-18-1

All rights reserved. No part of this publication may be reproduced or transmitted in any form or by any means, electronic or mechanical, including photography, recording, or any information storage or retrieval system, without permission in writing from the publisher. The book is sold subject to the condition that it shall not, by way of trade or otherwise, be lent, resold or otherwise circulated without the publisher's prior consent in any form of binding or cover other than that in which it is published and without a similar condition, including this condition, being imposed on the subsequent purchaser.

COVER IMAGE: *Rainwater Barrel* © *Dawn Hudson | Dreamstime.com*
COVER DESIGN & TYPESETTING: *Siobhán Hutson*
Printed in Ireland by Sprint Print

*Salmon Poetry gratefully acknowledges the support of
The Arts Council / An Chomhairle Ealaoín*

*For my family Abigail Joffe, Rowan and Jesse
and my extended family with love*

Acknowledgments

I would like to thank the editors of the following publications, in which some of these poems first appeared: *Cyphers, Force 10, Poetry Ireland Review, Idir Chruach is Chuan, Revival Poetry Journal, The SHOp, The Sligo Broadsheet* and the Kerry anthologies *Cúm* and *Breacadh*.

I would also like to acknowledge the support of Leland Bardwell, Paddy Bushe, Moya Cannon, the late Michael Donaghy, the late Mícheál Fanning, Eiléan Ní Chuilleanáin, and Macdara Woods and all who kept asking when is your book coming out?

Special thanks to Jessie and Siobhán at Salmon Poetry.

Thanks likewise to Sandra Landers for casting an eye over my manuscript and to my local writers' group for camaraderie in the craft.

I am grateful to Kerry County Council who awarded me a number of writing bursaries down through the years.

Special thanks to my wonderful family whose support made the book possible.

Contents

Nature	11
Ventry and Beyond	12
Tools	13
Coup de Foudre	14
York Street Cameo	15
A Manly Experience	18
Meditation in a Conil de la Frontera Café	20
Sunset	22
In Your Arms	23
Horses, People	24
Lapwings	25
The Rain Barrel	26
Merlin	27
Hooded Crow	29
Stage Fright	30
Vision	31
Onions	32
Valentine	33
Two Trees	34
Folktale	35
At Glaise Bheag	36
My Heart	37
Because	38
The News from Ballybunion	39
On attending a lecture on Bob Dylan by Michael Gray	40
Launching the Festival	41
Encounter	42
Nicknames	44

November	45
Whale Watcher	46
Identity	47
One for Sorrow	48
The Lesson	49
Jesse	51
On Being Distracted	53
West with the Night by Beryl Markham	54
Car	55
Rowan	57
Blonde Moment	58
Overdue	59
Seed-saver	60
Never	61
Lawn at Kilmatead	62
Dead Man's Hand	63
A Father Reminisces	64
Like Father Like Son	65
Resettlement	66
Songlines	67
Tom	68
Barbershop	69
Letting Go	70
Holiday	71
Learning to Cycle	72
The Chauffeur Explains	73
Returning	74
Sea Currency	75
Nursing Home	76

Nature

Above my head
grape vines under glass,
the green flare of growth
clothing the long stem
in sunlight and shadow
of a May morning.

Outside, just feet away,
where the black ink of winter
pools on the roots
of reed and bog iris
translucent green shoots appear
hour on hour.

The season
asserts herself,
both outdoors and in.
My son, all of a sudden fifteen,
my height, my shoe size,
the physique of a welterweight.

How I didn't hear his voice break
I don't know. Perhaps
because it occurred
when the raw light
of bud and leaf was so
blindingly centre stage.

Much later I realised
his was the voice
of a second man
in a house
where previously
one man lived.

Ventry and Beyond

Have you ever observed, particularly when driving,
quiet roads in the countryside are better for this —
how certain fixed objects — trees, telephone poles, fences —
can give the impression they are moving too?

The giant willows on the road up from the cross, for example.
One glimpse of the car has them jostling for position.
Then — strength in numbers — they form a small crowd.
Yet when I draw level they are stiff and immobile.

I'm not fooled though: I've seen their bones
in the x-ray light of November, December, January.
I figure — their near-death look notwithstanding —
they remember a time, when, like the district's old men,

when possibly they were old men themselves,
they were able to ramble the neighbourhood
without worrying about being a hazard to road users,
what side to walk on or when to jump into the ditch.

Tools

There's a countryman living in my tool-shed.
He's been there for years,
sleeps on the carpet in the corner
that crumbles into tiny pieces at my touch.
The door's wheezy rasp
announces his comings and goings.
Though I'm not sure if what I'm hearing
aren't his lungs, banjaxed from long nights
on the floor inhaling damp, creosote fumes, paint.
He does a decent job keeping an eye on the tools,
the farm, forestry and garden tools especially,
is reborn each time he hands me the sledge or the slasher.
He says they want to be admired, touched,
lifted from their dusty slumber into daylight,
cradled by the warmth and heartbeat of a human hand.

Each time he hands me one of these peaceful weapons
from out of the shed's interior gloaming
I feel a swelling in my chest,
particularly if it has a handle or shaft of ash or hickory.
Occasionally he unfurls his angel wings
and we raise a mug of tea
to honour the hammer, mell, mattock and tamper,
the tree-snedding clearing axe,
the bow saw and the pruning saw,
the billhook, loppers and sickle,
the spade, shovel, fork and rake,
the cut flat file bastard, the spokeshave, the hand brace,
the jack plane, mole wrench, monkey strainer and gin wheel.

Coup de Foudre

From the off I should have guessed that our proposed
dolphin trip from the marina in Dingle —
a glittering mirror-flash of yachts and sailing boats
tinkling gently in the breezy mid-morning air —
was likely to result in a sudden and astonishing happening

given that the craft at our disposal was little other
than a simple shell of propeller driven fibreglass,
which even a landlubber like me could see,
skimmed the waves with about as much nautical alacrity
as a sombrero-wearing unicyclist at sea in a hubcap.

At least I'd taken the precaution of bringing a life-jacket,
a man-made preserver of life, which inflates like a lung
when it hits water (as mysteriously as a lung itself inflates).
It held all my vital organs warm and snugly-belted in
in its peculiar, loving, blood-orange embrace,

an embrace I forgot once on open water
but which thrilled me again when Fungi the dolphin,
out of nowhere, surfaced alongside the boat,
the fabric of his sumptuous curved back
within touching distance of my outstretched fingers.

In an instant I was love-drunk and incoherent.
In fact, I almost fell overboard with the excitement.
I wondered about diving in and risking propeller-chop
so I could be with my new-found friend a little longer
but I soon realised the passion I was feeling

like a sickness couldn't possibly be reciprocated,
was, in any case, an infatuation that in time would
unravel itself from the bundle of knots in my stomach,
dart away like little fishes or be absorbed into my bloodstream
where such feelings swim until they fade and are forgotten.

York Street Cameo

It's Christmas week and I'm getting out of the city
to spend the season of goodwill with my mother
and siblings in deepest County Monaghan.
The car boot is packed solid with shopping,
bananas and stuff from the veg shop on Wexford Street,
a backpack with my clothes and runners,
and my beloved, 6-stringed, jumbo acoustic guitar.
The guitar, a Suzuki, is in its coffin, padlocked.
The coffin is a satin-lined, almost triangular
wooden box weighing about two stone,
into which any sleeping baby Jesus would comfortably fit.

Because the Corpo has recently painted double yellow lines
on the road outside the flat and the lock on the boot
of my antique Toyota is only for show
the plan is to park directly outside 29F,
race up to the third floor,
then get back down to the car *rapido*.

It's the hour before the evening rush.
I'm on the lookout for suspicious looking types.
That means anyone not in a car or on a bike
because basically we live on a drive-only, cycle-only street.
Only College of Surgeons' students risk walking
the short trot from the Green to the college entrance
directly opposite our flat.

I make a big display of locking the car,
likewise turning the key in the boot
to demonstrate to anyone watching
how securely locked the vehicle is,
and then, as soon as I'm out of sight
I tear up the stairs.
It's no problem – running everyday
puts coiled springs into the calf muscles.

Anyway, I'm in the dark vaulting upwards
from landing to landing; at most it's 45 seconds to my flat door.
Then it's *open sesame*, down the corridor
to the carrier bags I left on the kitchen table,
and back out and down the stairs two or three at a time.

I'm away from the scene, what, three minutes at most.
The car is still straddling those yellow lines
and parallel to the kerb, as I left it.
The scene is quiet also, nary a sinner or innocent in sight,
though cars, vans, buses, pedestrians, cyclists
enter, cross and then exit my picture view of pavement trees
and railing shrubs at the Stephen's Green end.

I unlock the door, am just about to sit in and turn the key
when the thought crosses my mind. Better check the boot!

There's no need to reprise my bad acting charade
of a moment ago now that I'm about to drive off
so I just go to the back of the car, glance around
in a cursory fashion and yank the boot open.

Of course the boot is empty, completely empty.
My guitar, rucksack, bags, everything gone.
It takes a while for me to realise what has happened
but when I do I'm suddenly alert,
scanning the tenement's façade for signs of life,
a shadow or net curtain moving across a window,
the heel of a shoe vanishing into one of the hallways.
I'm looking for someone, anyone, who might have seen
the scumbag who walked away with all my gear.
That's when I see him, the under-sized fella
in a dark sweatshirt smoking in a doorway down the block.
Hell, if he was there 5 minutes ago
then surely he must have witnessed the whole episode.

Straightaway I go up to him and tell him what's after happening
in the most nasally, inner-city Dublin accent I can muster.
I make sure to say I've been living in number 29,

with my mother and my youngest brother, *for ten years*,
that I can't believe lads here would rob one of their own.

He takes a drag from his cigarette like I don't exist,
then looks down at my shoes for longer than necessary.
'You're a copper,' he spits, 'you've got copper's feet.'
I'm close enough to smell his sweat, except he's not sweating, I am.

O-kay, I say to myself, now this I don't believe.
I'm whispering now and nodding at the car.
'If I'm a cop, then why am I driving that heap of shit?'
He ponders this, blinks once or twice, takes another puff.
The fag's burning ember flares briefly, then dies.
He flicks the butt at the ground, crushes it with the sole of his shoe.

'Wait here,' he says, and with that he is gone.
Five minutes later I hear footsteps in the hallway.
The first thing I see is the nose of my guitar case.
Then he emerges with my rucksack and other stuff.

It happened the way I've told you.
Except that now I think I should have acknowledged his gesture,
shaken his hand or somehow demonstrated
the brotherhood I felt for him.

The best I think I managed was –
I don't blame you. I'd have done the same in your shoes.

A Manly Experience

It's the winter of '78,
the clubhouse in Hospital Lane, Islandbridge.
I'm just out of the showers, naked
(except for towel draped shoulder to navel)
on the concrete-cold, run-off plinth
that rises from the floor.
One of the senior men emerges from the steam
and without warning eyeballs me –
'Are you homosexual?' he says.
It isn't so much the 'Are you,
Aren't you?' in the question,
but the way he articulates the word homosexual
loudly, utterly without innuendo or shame,
just asking, wondering, curious,
in front of so many other, if not naked,
then half-naked men and boys,
every syllable clearly enunciated
with passionate, sexual confidence
in his rich, south-Dublin brogue.

I know he isn't; he boasts about bored housewives
as we lash out sub-six minute miles
on the 12 mile lap, what he does to them
in front rooms in Dundrum and Ballinteer
when the husband is at work.
I've seen his wife on the team bus.

I don't have a girlfriend that he can see.
My girlfriends are invisible. So what?
I'm not a homo
I never thought I was a homo
but his question –
his genuine concern at the opportunities
for sex that I am missing,
whether homo or hetero,

whether boy or girl,
his faith in sex, his ambition for sex,
his refreshing honesty and absence of guilt about sex
wherever or with whom —

I look at his Tuesday evening
waist-down nakedness
hanging there for all to see
amongst all the other
man and boy naked declarations
in the clubhouse —
(squad training is Tuesdays and Thursdays,
turnout is always better on a Tuesday)

All this stripped-down, body-worshipping,
common or garden, road-honed nakedness
not seen anywhere except in club
changing rooms nationwide.
Surely that's something to pronounce upon,
invisible or not.

Meditation in a Conil de la Frontera Café

Rain in a Spanish seaside town that could be Brighton
and almost immediately the torrent of tourists is swept
clean from the streets. The smell of relief rises faintly
from pavements as shops close up early, their owners
retreat to a quiet corner in the Café Bar Oasis.

It's not the rolling TV news I'm watching but a silent film,
a picturescape of images: crowd protests in Syria; a tasselled
assembly of square-shouldered Cuban politicos; a South
American tornado's demolition site that somehow recalls
that mask of alienation I once wore on an 80s Brighton street.

In my hand the latest edition of Graham Greene's Brighton Rock.
Fifty thousand visitors a day to that south-coast resort
back when the Boy Pinkie and his cronies began to stroll
about on the piers and promenades of the great writer's imagination.
Does such an underworld exist in this old sea-dog *puerto* I wonder?

Up town the clock tower tolls on the hour.
A surfer in shades and sandals walks in (very un-Brighton),
followed by a girl with love hearts sequinned
onto the back pockets of her jeans. Both disappear upstairs.
For a moment I want to be him, young and in love like that.

It's still raining outside. Warm rain, not like
Irish rain or Brighton rain which soaks to the skin.
Until now I thought there wasn't an umbrella in the whole of Spain.
If fact, I was certain there wasn't even a word
for it in their language but now I hear otherwise.

Para agua/for water. It expresses perfectly
the Spaniard's inclination to meet the world head on
(see bullfighting) without any euphemistic entanglements,
which goes no way to explaining why in our 1930s
bright town a cut-throat razor was known as a Brighton umbrella.

Back on the box TV4's Marta Sánchez is reporting
a bomb scare from outside Barcelona's *Sagrada Familia*
but I'm elsewhere, surely not Brighton, and the sun's coming out
and I want to settle the bill, put the book in my pocket,
perhaps walk to the seafront and watch the waves crash in.

Sunset

This is the pits.
It's only half three
(of a January afternoon)
and already the sun is fast
disappearing behind the ridge
above *Cill Mhic a' Domhnaigh*.

The precious light,
which all afternoon pooled
a cheery optimism onto the living
room floor, is going down the sink-hole.

Half a mile away
on a neighbour's farm,
every square rood and perch,
every ditch, dyke, drain and dug-out
is aflare with the flames of a fantastic fire.

A mile further on
the village is similarly ablaze.
Here the late sun unrolls itself on silk bay water,
climbs the pier, leaves embers smouldering on the village green.

We can't move the mountain without dynamite
but we can, as one neighbour suggested, get the hell out
from under its raven wings before the white coats come knocking.

In Your Arms
for Abigail Joffe

When I'm in your arms do I think about love?
In your embrace I don't think about love,
in fact I try not to think at all,
for I fear that thinking overwhelms feeling, true feeling,
interferes with beauty's expression of loveliness.
When you wrap me in your arms I feel love,
I feel you; I feel love and you together.
I feel the oh in love, the oh in now, the oh in you,
the ohs unquantifiable in you and love and now together.
When you hold me, love is nothing else but you and now
and now and you and now and now and now.

Horses, People

We walk the road between church and graveyard
in the old style, on foot behind the undertaker's car,
our sheer numbers holding up the traffic behind us
for the ten or fifteen minutes it takes to reach the turn.

In a treeless field on the right, half a dozen grazing horses
(a bay mare, a chestnut, some piebald ponies)
lift their heads as one and approach the hedge.
They watch our passing with those deep brown, otherworldly
    equine eyes

that see us and look through us at the same time.
The procession moves forward, cars pass me on the inside.
I'm in the middle of the road looking back at them
while the world we've peopled moves on to bury its dead.

When I turn to follow the cortège, the horses too turn away.
The hedge dissolves to bramble, hawthorn once again.
Horses, people, for the time we are together go back to being
just horses in a field grazing, just people on a road walking.

Lapwings

I brought you news of lapwings
knowing you'd understand
how precious their sighting was to me,
a flock settling nervously on those
sandy estuary fields that ring the bay
near where the graveyard's inhabitants lie.
I counted ten or twenty one day,
forty or fifty the day after.

These sometime visitors fill
the land-locked, Wiltshire countryside
round where you were born
with their small quavering hearts
on days when sunlight and wind-chill
dance fleet-of-foot together
on that county's chipped mosaic floor.

I've seen them often – that wing flash
of white on black is unmistakeable –
rise up in low, wind-driven clouds
from stubble crop fields, flinty up slopes
where barley and winter wheat are still grown.
I've listened to the drifting flock
cry out to one another:
head west, head west.

Once protected by an Act of Parliament
I envy them their strut and stance
upon marsh or mud, hill or headland.
They have what we most want,
a wing-flickering mind
ever alert to what might happen
where it is coldest, wettest, windiest.
They have the keenest of eyes for both earth and sky.

The Rain Barrel

You left in a downpour.
I watched the rain barrel fill
and overflow.
Spit formed
on the gutter's lip
as underneath a stem of froth
grew and flowered in an instant.

When the wind died
the stem collapsed
but not before
a thousand water seeds
were broadcast in a sweep
across the yard.

Merlin

Do you remember boys, the unseasonably mild
day I picked you up from the school bus
– before the clocks went back –
when a merlin appeared beside the car
and briefly flew alongside as we motored home?
Your mother and I were trying to uncouple,
reclaim our individuality,
live less on auto-pilot.

Only the glass on the driver's side
and the stanchion nearest the steering wheel
came between us and the bird
– pale grey and creaturely –
as it hung there motionless,
no more than an arm's length away.

Outside, the hedgerow's script
of yellow and green tumbled backwards.
The hawk, framed in the light of the window
continued to accompany the car
even as we drifted on the cambered road
and the bend ahead drew dangerously near.

I looked at you both, took my foot
off the accelerator, slowed the car.
In the quietness trees, telephone poles,
fuchsia bushes, rolled past.
The bird, with rounded wings
vibrating in the wind, flew on.

There were things I wanted to say
about what we adults were going through
(for example did uncoupling mean splitting up?)
but I couldn't bring myself to disturb the car's
post-school reverie, change the look on your faces
for the sake of a few ill-chosen words,
a story even I didn't know the end of.

Besides, the hawk was here,
a once-off that likely would never return.
Had you even noticed it,
the wonder of it so close to the car,
its speed and position relative to ours
fixed yet moving, like a star in the night sky?
Were you not amazed by its jet power,
its manoeuvrability, its tiny foot-long frame?

We skimmed past a neighbour's drive.
I touched the brake as a precaution,
felt the car respond to the pressure of my foot.
The bird reacted, banked right,
swept itself up over the hedge
as easily as dust before a brush
and vanished from sight.

That left me, as the bend came and went,
pondering the question I had no answer to.
And a galvanised gate through which
I caught a glimpse of the meadow
where I imagined I could see
the dot of the hawk's flight fade to nothing.

Hooded Crow

Low tide attracts them, as it does me.
A long beach exposed, no two days the same.
The one I meet, a regular here,
is holding his ground: a strip of sand
west of the estuary and the metal bridge.

And yes, I've studied his pre-lift off routine –
the pinprick of light in his night-black eye;
how he sinks, clicks, locks his body weight
onto deceptively thin, biro spring legs.

There are others of course, furtive, shifty,
who likewise patrol the shore in two-tone garb.
I saw one boyo take the wind escalator skywards.
He came back down the same way he went up.

Stage Fright

I feel it in my chest first,
a trapped bird flapping his wings.
Then a piston, as in a car engine
or bicycle pump, which up till now

had been holding back, applies pressure
and my heart rises, falls, rises again.
Now I have lungs that won't inflate
and a stomach that wants only to growl.

Meanwhile the aforementioned bird
who followed the light and found my throat
has mistaken my tongue for a worm
and let rip his single rough vowel.

Vision
for Joanna Keane

I met her while cycling to the village shop
the morning the British & Irish Lions
were hammering the Wallabies flatter than flat
in that decisive test match down under.

I braked on gravel, skidded to a stop.
Straddled the crossbar, was kissed on the cheek.
Before we said our goodbyes
she told me she was heading to a beachside

restaurant I'm absolutely certain didn't exist
to guzzle raw oysters, sip flutes of salt water.
Three times I asked her for the name of the place.
Three times I was told but didn't understand.

Onions

I found the onions at ten yard intervals when
I was measuring my stride against the beach's usual length.
The tide had tossed them onto the sand
and then retreated, leaving each onion
at odds with the ordinary wisps of seaweed,
shells and pebbles otherwise aground on the shore.

They had been polished by some turbulent force
or combination of forces involving an abrasive
and the application of a thin oily gloss.
Some were bruised and leathery, with peeling skin,
others had found their equilibrium in a sand-nest
or were lolling to one side with root strings trailing.

I scanned the shoreline until I found one
that was most true to its condition,
had the peculiar size to weight ratio I was looking for,
sat easily in the palm of my hand. When I bowled it
down the beach it rolled like a severed head,
landed against a clump of weed with an audible groan.

Valentine

At school, despite the love instinct
Valentine felt from his first teacher,
he disappointed at penmanship and joined up writing.
His own name, in capitals at first,
never flowed, was reduced to a trickle.
The later attempts at his signature,
this essence of who he was, were forgeries.
They fool the tax official
and the border guard, he said, but they don't fool me.

Hence the cards. And the month
he chose to deliver them,
in which his love, if that's what it is,
is revealed in clean, naked lines
in every thicket and hedgerow,
in the bare crown of every tree
and over the bay, where the flight of Brent geese
is written in immaculate longhand
in sweat and blood, ink and tears.

Two Trees

These two trees were never going
to thrive or survive on the same acre.
When the kids began referring to them
as mammy and daddy trees
I knew it was only a question of time
before there'd be trouble.

The chestnut ended up in a gap
in the hedge. He's the figurative one,
all shoulders and swagger.
If he could he'd go walkabout, tramp long miles
on narrow country roads to freshen the mind,
feel a different geography under his feet.

The mountain ash found herself in the wood
surrounded by others of her kind.
She's all mood, gangly
and self-effacing, abstract almost.
Her life force is the sap stirring
in her gut, gentle breezes.

I hear them from my bed,
laying into each other on certain nights.
At first it's just flailing about, insults,
a branch being broken, but then it gets serious.
It's been going on so long I'm almost relieved
when they start kicking and punching one another.

Folktale

Under the light
of a winter-low sun the other day,
on the road they call *an bothar bán*,
I came upon a line of eight
or ten tall, pale-skinned figures
proceeding slowly towards me.
They carried themselves
with a kind of man-grace
not seen round here
since the days of old Jack Manning,
who, before he died, I used regularly
meet along this very road
pushing his ancient bicycle
home from the shop
with bread and milk
hanging from the handlebars
in a plastic bag.

The figures stepped into the ditch
to avoid the car and let me pass,
gave me a friendly, long-limbed wave.
Of course, I returned their greeting,
but I made sure to check them out
one last time in my one-eyed,
rear-view mirror.
They were moving
with the same lack of urgency
I sometimes feel in my bones
through the withered grasses
of the roadside's
rushy margin.

At Glaise Bheag

A council of Spanish poets in Castilian plumage
address us from the top table. In Spanish.
They clearly haven't left Spain yet,
are oblivious to their land-that-time-forgot surroundings,
to the Three Sisters visible in the window behind them
bent to their eternal task, to Pierce Feirtír's Iberian connections.
Yet somehow they connect.

It is May, mid-afternoon and hot. There is a pool
of silence to be filled and their words fill it.
These are hot rhythms from a hot country.
Who would not welcome it?
Who would not wish to be immersed in it?

The snores of the elderly English gent are an undertow
in a dream of cold water, clear as the Atlantic.
Each breath held is a little death,
each reawakening a gasp for air.
Is he dead? Is he alive?
Does it matter if he never resurfaces
when at the table is a poet
who says he can stop time in his poems?

My Heart
after Osip Emilevich Mandelstam

Glory be. The fog's lifted.
I can breathe at last. Open my lungs.
The flutter of wings on my heart
last night was a warning, a warning.

What about that trip to town
I promised myself? The people
are waiting. I must see the people,
exchange a paragraph or two of banter.

I'll want noise as well. Machine noise.
And the whiff of petrol fumes up my nostrils.
That and people on Main Street looking,
the weight of someone's eyes on me.

I'm not invisible just yet, thank God!
I have money, euro coins, notes.
If necessary I can flash my wallet,
my putative identity papers in fake leather.

That surely will light up a smile
on the waitress's face in my regular haunt.
I'll ask for the usual, a double espresso,
with hot milk on the side,

water in a glass, and we'll laugh
together about how predictable life is.
She'll stand at my table, a perfect fit
for her skin, holding my heart in her hands.

Because

Because of that handshake and the bolt
of lightning she kept wrapped up in her fist
for moments like this, and the selection of murder mysteries,
thrillers and literary suspenses in the bookshop's
Vital Titles section on shelves at her back.

Because of the wraith who hovered beside her
at the door, who matched her stride for stride on the street
with a footfall that never touched the pavement
and was always there in the crowded pub
attracting the barman's attention.

Because of her country where the body
of a dead poet can lie for days in the city morgue
unclaimed and unidentified because there are
so few readers of modern poetry around.

Because of catastrophe's shake of the head
and the dark star of an old suffering
that lingered in a half-told story
back when she was a little girl
and her father was her father
and there was nothing, nothing she could do.

The News from Ballybunion
for Clem Cairns

I saw two halves of a strand below a cliff
open like a sheet of old newspaper.
On it I read the news from Ballybunion,
a story made oddly compelling by the passage of time.

Hung-over, doped and dumb, last night's
whiskey shots in John B's had done for me.
I'd slept in a coffin, the three foot high roof-space
of your camper van, in a castle car park.

The drive over hadn't improved matters
though I wondered at a stretch of open country
treeless as a steeplechase course
and the brick by brick symmetry
of those caravan parks as we neared the sea.

We stripped off – there was no one around –
and left our grown up bodies in a heap on the sand.
The boys we once were looked at one another and ran.
The water was as you'd expect. Torture.
Afterwards we thanked God our wives are beautiful, as you do.

On attending a lecture on Bob Dylan by Michael Gray

I wouldn't read too much into it but one and a half hours
swinging between the ditch and the continuous white
on switch back roads, the tape hot from overplaying
Sad-eyed Lady, Visions of Johanna, Absolutely Sweet Marie.

On stage at St. John's the biographer mesmerises me
with his pacy walk and talk: Dylan in sleepy Duluth,
housebound and squirming;
running messages to Zimmer's bread store in Hibbing
he sacks the town's clapboard mythologies, takes what he can.

At 16 he gets the hell out to cram a lifetime's Eng. Lit.
into one Minneapolis semester.
In the early years of that Greenwich Village decade
he's writing five songs a day.

But back to our friend who, tongue-bereft,
meets his hero back-stage at Manchester or Earls Court
and unable to think of anything but the line from Idiot Wind:

they say I shot a man named Gray
and took his wife to Italy

says cheerfully, 'My wife says you can take her to Italy anytime'.
Our friend missed the nineties writing the book.
I can see how that might happen.

Launching the Festival

May again, when culture's red tide,
swims most forcibly in the blood.
The narrow road above the creek
where I park the car serpentines
down to the base of a cliff
and a harbour behind a wall of rock
where the odyssey of Brendan began.

On the pier eight girls in monks' habits
carry a blue *papier-mâché* whale,
school children stand next to a *naomhóg*,
hide tin whistles under uniforms.
Later they'll play the tune
they spent the week rehearsing.

In a triangle of sunlight women spread
the weight of small talk amongst themselves.
The *sean-nós* singer, the parish priest
and the local doctor bestow their blessings
on a ceremony I didn't know
I needed until this moment.

Before the crowd breaks up to leave,
a Palestinian singer-in-exile gifts us a song
from her country. Her voice is strong, compassionate.
It conveys a suffering that surely every heart here feels.
We nod in understanding, gather ourselves,
drift solemnly away in ones, twos, threes.

Encounter

I'd just formed an orderly queue of one
when she turned up — our town's street ghost —
and parked herself at my shoulder.
Her stance said: Seriously Pissed Off!
'I'm looking for a husband,'
she growled to no one in particular.

The poster in my hand curled visibly.
It advertised a lunchtime poetry reading
which very few people, men or women,
drunk or sober, were going to attend
even if the lads here allowed it be displayed
in their uncluttered shop-front window —
tho' herself might turn up to accompany
the poet's words with a grumble if a glass was going.

Her face was swollen, her eyes raw.
I watched her with fatal interest
cease swaying long enough
to ask the fella behind
the desk if he was married.
His answer only encouraged her.

'I want a husband for Christmas,' she demanded,
as if Christmas was around the corner
(it was early September),
as if one of us would likely volunteer
to give up that special morning
nearly four months hence
to be unwrapped in her kitchen,
a human bundle of spangly paper
tied off with a ribbon and bow.

The boys telegraphed me a look.
I glanced at the door. Closed.
It was a joint, full-in-the-face salvo
meant for the two of us, now irrevocably joined:
'Nicholas! He's your man! Saint Nicholas!'

The saddest thing about the whole episode was that
she was too blitzed to bear her share of the weight,
much less notice how I staggered
under the load heaped upon my shoulders.

Nicknames

The first, Nick the Greek,
was a shadow name,
the kind that creeps with us
from adolescence to adulthood
inspired – if I recollect rightly –
by the oily character
of a TV mini-series whose anchovy
image confirmed the view of
Mediterranean men we had back then,
all of them fishy in a sexual way,
criminally dodgy, obsequious to boot.

Number two, Nicolopolis Philodopolis,
was more experimental,
its genesis an engineer's laboratory humour.
The syllables were Greek and hard to swallow.
It ran with a long stride of awkward Os
and tho' it ended in peace was anything but.

This one's second wind I credit
to the bus-sized enthusiasms
of a college athletic team on tour –
all of ancient and modern Greece
in a ten day odyssey,
and that mechanical minded lad
who stress-tested his laughs.

Near the Parthenon I saw
the Athenian body armour
of hoplites who head-butted
the Persians back to the sea.
I conjured it into
the message of victory
Philippedes ran with
when he covered the distance
from Marathon to home.

November

The wind imp runs on the roof
The reed sips from the soakaway pit

The pheasant squats in the scutch
The nettle undresses

The seal keeps her promise
The wave smiles back

The kittiwake, the kestrel and the kite surfer
The fish box, the lobster pot and the *naomhóg*

The bottle bank winks a Cyclops eye
The street light shivers in a net of rain

Whale Watcher

Sunday morning. Buddha of the cliff edge
sitting cross-legged on a stone wall,
binoculars in one hand, coffee in a thermos cup.

In her quartering of the water for bait balls,
kittiwakes, gulls in a frenzied knot of feeding
and the shadowy foot print
a Minke whale leaves on the surface,
she shows me what to look for.

Ahoy, at twelve o'clock, are the Blaskets,
charting the ruffled waters of the Sound,
the wind full in their majestic land-sails.
The big island alone has so many features
from which to hook a sight-line:

the summit they call *The Crow*,
heather that blooms like a red flower
in this strange October light,
and below right a slice of cliff
caught in a frozen dive to the ocean bed.

I kneel to rest my elbows on the low wall
and focus on a stretch of ocean.
Time passes in such worship.
The whales gift us their creaturely
presence in a silent prayer.

Identity

Up the boreen
first house on the right
Tigh an Átha

white gable, red windows
where the river crosses the road
or the road crosses the river

is where you'll find me most days
In this up-slope, land hollow
spring arrives early, late or not at all

a frost brings worms to the surface
birds leave their tracings
in the sky

The front door is open
a column of sunlight stands
like a visitor on the slate floor

On the CD player
my latest musical heroine
tells urban stories

of a loud decade
as if exhorting me to feel
as strongly about my generation

A jet rumbles overhead
filling the sky with its own
importance

Last week in the car
I surprised a hare
into playing its invisible game

This is who we are
a ghost of light and shade
the stranger seen from within

One for Sorrow

He's outside the window, attention-seeking again,
scouting for trouble. This time in the wych elm.
The solitary magpie, my tree-hopping, head-wrecking friend.
Somehow I always know when he's but a wing-beat away.

This goes back a long way, to the dreamtime of youth.
Then, as now, he was the solo flyer, the busiest bird
in the hood and I was drawn to the blues of his bluesman song,
the throat-rattle of his one-track repertoire.

We meet occasionally as one loner-companion to sorrow
and sadness recognising another. It's then I recall
what years ago in the Phoenix Park flew from a child's rhyme
to perch provocatively in a young man's mind.

The Lesson

This twinning of two families — one living abroad
and one in Ireland, see — on a skiing holiday
was a neutral act, a truce, a back-to-basics
tutorial in how to stand up for oneself.

What better locale could there be for brothers
living in the slit of a wrongly remembered wound
to rebalance what went askew in their teenage years
and never fully righted itself.

The day they drive to the mountains they give thanks;
there is snow, or machines that do the work of God.
The lives of the TV weathermen can be spared,
the off-camera guns put away for another year.

Mitterbach is low key in an Austrian way,
has all the ski apparatus two Irishmen will ever need:
groaning steel, the ghostly furniture of buildings dressed in white,
a Jacob's ladder of chair and drag lifts
carrying the snow obsessed into a mountaintop heaven.

Alas, the oldest brother must suffer the beginner's class,
a whizz-kid *ski meister* dispensing counter-intuitive advice:
*ride the blade of a knife — trust its stopping power,
lean away from safety and into the abyss,*

when what he wants most is to be twenty again.
But wait, by mid-week he has found his snow-legs,
won the argument with his skis. Now, finally, he can
warrior-up in his battle dress, ride his skis down

the forest trail to the clearing where his brother waits.
The light is sharp between the trees, the voices
of far-off skiers float high on the thin air.
Underfoot are the conditions that mark out

the site where their understanding will be reached.
Afterwards, he climbs up out of the snow
to shake hands with his brother and breathe pure air.
He spits, a door in his head open, the winter light beckoning.

Jesse

1.

Caught flat-footed as you cannon-shot
from your mother's womb
I watched you whizz past my outstretched hands.
Equally badly positioned
by the unreliable ripple blur of memory
I cannot be sure
if you hit the floor before the doc
scooped you up in his arms
and untangling a cord twisted like telephone flex
handed you back in one piece
to your euphoric, exhausted mother.

2.

Dawn-snug and dozing as you crept
out of sight on the bedroom floor
as elusive and self-possessed as an early cuckoo
calling from the here, there and everywhere of the room –
until the ominous seepage of silence
warned our fogged brains too late.
How the after-notes of your ladder-dive
down the stairs pierced our hearts!

3.

At four it's obvious you've inherited anger,
your face contorts back to the primate.
What a heart-rage and cheeks hot to touch,
though I've high hopes a sporting future
will reduce it to pitch-sized proportions.

4.

The frame of the sycamore animates adventure.
One day we'll *crannóg* a tree house
inaccessible to adults, with footings on living beams
but for now we make do with a knotted hanging rope
and the swing I've sat you on.
Can you feel my hand on your back?
Collage of flesh and bone, summary of love.

On Being Distracted

Going out to pick gooseberries from prickly bushes
that survive in a clump of neglect
near the vegetable beds
my head fills at the tangle of bindweed
surging sunwards up the fruiting stems.

I should leave it alone. The stuff is more
animal than vegetable, has a steely attitude
to anything other than seasonal die-back.
Feeding those ligatures the merest of glances
only tightens its grip on my mind.

Toss an inch carelessly away
on a raised or hot bed,
and it will root in a day, periscope up,
asphyxiate the peas and climbing beans,
rip at my hands as I rip at it.

I see the weed lurking in every half acre site
let go to waste. I see white flowers
that blossom in the head
preparing new versions of itself
on earth we leave clear.

West with the Night by Beryl Markham

was the book I most wanted her to read
during our non-committal, on-off again
relationship that was based on collision
as much as anything else, though my recall
is not all single beds and mattresses on floors,
the wreckage of blankets thrown clear.

She shared a name with the aviator,
had tomboy good looks, wind-burnt cheeks,
but what made me doubly stupid
was the book's background noise,
the notion you could dog-ear
someone else's life at the interesting bits.

Her take off for seasonal work to an American
military base somewhere in Bavaria reprised
The Gull's shrieking trans-Atlantic 1930s flight
on a course hooked by a Cape Breton low,
the drone of a de Havilland motor
writing a new sentence on a blank sky,

so it made a kind of sense when a season later
we bumped into one another on O'Connell Bridge
during one of her swooping returns to the city,
and her suggestion of a trip to the Yugoslav coast
ignited the hope of something physical where
the sea was mapped a cartographer's blue.

I travelled with the book's expression of someone
she couldn't be; air scout for elephant guns,
East African racehorse trainer to a beloved *Pegasus*,
as far as Sarajevo, where she went west.
We were to meet in Munich. I skipped that bit,
figuring one day we'd pick up where we left off.

Car

You remember the Triumph Herald estate we found
comatose on the Pembroke Road, four flabby tyres,
moss on window seals, hardly perfect mechanical order,
which the owner valued less than the sum of spare parts.

Worth salvaging for twenty quid you said it was;
sister to the saloon version you were driving then,
the first car I was to own outright if we could make it go.
If not, well, we could always cannibalise it.

In our collective time we'd sat in some old bangers:
you in Bubble-cars, Consuls and a fleet of Beetles,
me in Anglias, Morris Minors and unfashionable Fiats,
and make no bones about it they were bone-shakers all,

clapped out motors prone to fainting fits, seizures
and sitting down on the job. Rust-buckets with a short
life expectancy, makeshifted by Isopon and string.
Some were hand-me-downs, passed from righteous uncle

to black sheep. There was one as bond (or was it bounty?)
the cops took a curious interest in. It's true I never
had any illusions they'd ever be family cars,
with two ever-present parents up front,

2.4 children in the back even if it was in such crates
that I honed my driving skills
(hand brake turns in the belly of the lane,
emergency stops an inch from a matchbox on the tarmac).

I can still feel the bolt of electricity that
my hands transmitted to the steering wheel
when the Enniskerry bus pulled out unexpectedly
and my swerve to miss butterfly-kissed it.

I well remember too, my Morris Minor moment
when the right front wheel skewed inward
(it topped its thole pin in a pothole),
and both car and I waltzed ungainly across the oncoming traffic.

From our perspective Triumph Heralds were solid,
honest models, with distinctive livery built to last,
so surely we could make this 1100 go?
With yours parked nose to nose with the other

I opened a bonnet that hinged forward, not back,
a bonnet that hung on leathery ligaments,
double-jointed like my brother's elbow and cleared
the carburettor's reedy valve (one you lifted

every night to curb my father's midnight flits),
while you clamped jump-leads — untangled from
a snake-pit knot on your passenger floor —
to both batteries and somehow resuscitated

the engine sufficiently to limp home. One morning
a week or so later, with the battery flat again,
it occurred to me yours would always be
the one car I could rely upon to spook life into mine.

Rowan

We named you thus long before
our rooting back into the past
discovered that the clan symbol
for your Scottish McLachlan ancestors
was indeed the hardy mountain rowan.

Nourished by love it confirmed your place
among the many generations of spear-carriers
lined up in loose formations behind you.
The right name for a whip of a boy
home-born under a high mountain.

The first nights were fragile:
while you slept beside me in the vast bed
and your mother rested in another downstairs,
I lay sleepless in a night swoon
watching your chest rise and fall.

At an age best measured in halves, not wholes,
you navigate the sitting room rubble of Matchbox cars,
wooden tenders and farmyard animals.
Surprised at every step and turn by rediscovered toys
that scarcely a moment ago ghosted from your sight,
by the pieces of the jigsaw puzzle that reassure you that you fit.

You're a stayer, curious about words and their meanings,
starting out on language's long, long run.
Look out for the family vernacular on your paternal
grandmother's side, that lineage of the absurd,
the surreal and the playful that burns like fire on the tongue.

Child warrior, with the strength of years
strung across your home-made bow
you come in like fresh air and disarm.
I breathe you in like something seasonal and innate:
the scent of wild garlic, bluebells in a wood.

Blonde Moment

I had a blonde moment headlined the *Daily Telegraph*
of the woman who parked her Land-Rover in a lake.
Her excuse: in low light water glosses over,
looks like wet tarmac.

This is language as it is lived
by the 'Chelsea tractor' set,
a most expressive expression in womanly form,
photographed in the act, good-looking, sexy, vivacious,
confidently flaunting the fuck-up,
climbing out of a half-submerged jeep.

The flip side is a sub-editor in a Wapping newsroom
drooling over his brain wave. In the inky dawn
the city's buildings rise up like font on printer's plate.
Later, over a beer in an early house
he'll take credit for its circulation, for its common usage.

Overdue

August. Our second child is overdue.
In the garden the plum tree's laden branches
bring to mind the flare and ripple
of its April blossoming
that lit up the sky
when we were more than halfway there.

A display that came from soft explosions,
like those that break your belly's stretched skin
when the baby kicks, that leave me counting the seconds,
as one might do between thunder-shock and lightning strike,
so I might judge how long we have to wait.

Seed-saver

Blaithín, this early comer
bringer of new stories
seed-saver for old.
A man easy on the soil
ranked and titled
honoured above the rest.

Not the island's first blow-in
nor its last
but for all that he
might have been a time-traveller
back-tracking through time
crossing The Sound
beaching his craft on sheet metal sand
– bronze age man pitying his Neolithic predecessor –

Instead, spanning two worlds
he split the seedcase of that oral tradition
and season after season broadcast its essence
enabling new writers to record
the names of sea-caves
the lives of the drowned
the precise location of oat fields
a heady mixture of the half-forgotten and the half-remembered.

Never

in memory of Valerie Hone

She never ran out of anything.
There was always tea, ceremoniously poured,
egg and tomato sandwiches on goose-feather white,
the luxury of sponge cake, and a shrew-sized
jam spoon poking from the spout of a glazed pot.

We fought over the tricycle in the sloped passage,
burrowed under the sofa in the drawing room.
We never went upstairs.
We crossed the mill race to gather chestnuts.
Green air flushed city lead from our lungs.

There was sherry and money as the light faded
and so much we were never told.
An old man pressed sixpenny pieces into our hands;
for my mother he tellered a paper transaction.

She was the grandmother we never had.
She had pedigree, made amends.
I didn't want her to die.
She never did.

Lawn at Kilmatead
for Eamon Colman

Lazing about, layabout!
on grass that will never be a lawn
he's busy day-dreaming
about the croquet-smooth number one cut
the mower on his maternal side
and all the work a good lawn takes
work you cannot see.

Dead Man's Hand

in memory of Katherine Kavanagh

My seventh birthday fell on the day
your husband died
and from that day on we were linked
through grief and celebration
and the presents you bought me
marked time.

Later on you taught me
seven card stud, southern cross
with arpeggios of cards
ascending, descending
a flick here, a flick there
holding, passing, smoking.

I remember cards slurring off the deck
going for open-ended straights
chasing the blue
or superstitiously holding an ace
and an eight
to fill the dead man's hand.

A Father Reminisces

Remember when Galileo, not yet a year and a half
with everything in orbit around him
stood up on our bed early one morning
and putting himself between us and the fireball
raised his right hand to mirror a reflection out of wood
his body the gold paint to plain glass.

How years later the same *garsúinín*
told us the sun was the centre of the universe.

Like Father Like Son

You were always a great man with the axe
like father like son
fond of saying
I taught you everything you know not everything I know
descendant from Scottish nobility
great claymore wielding warriors
seeing off sassanachs at Culloden.

The time you hunted down wild goat in the Wicklow hills —
not like the highlands, boy.
Have you ever been to Scotland da?

Not much use to me now
all your power gone, manic power
weakened by cheap rot-gut plonk
excursions into the small hours
Lachlan son of Lachlan
turned to the English for title and estates in the south.

In Gortaforia I'm splitting logs by the cart-house
you're taking your ease in the sun
funny how the last time you wielded the axe
was the night your three young sons
barricaded their bedroom door
and lay in bed listening for footsteps on the stairs.

You were always a great man with the axe.

Resettlement

In perpetual rain we orient our geological time-map
by the ripple marks on horizontal sandstone;
once volcanic, then glacial.
But by what features will I, a veteran of three winters, adjust position?

I never answered when they asked,
'How long are you staying?' How could I?

All I know is I'm taking new bearings,
travelling from the smaller to the larger scale,
leaving this era of disused railways, rights of way, county boundaries,
to where I will put down time at the Prime meridian,
one foot in the west, one foot in the east,
align my body to its new co-ordinates,
but leave the spirit free to watch the rushes reclaim the deep-beds
and listen to the spider's song.

Songlines

Inch, a sea-meadow that stretches into infinity.
A strand that spans the contradictions between languages, and ages.

When I walk between the high water mark and the low
I am walking on sheet music swept clean.

It is in those hours between tides
that I can score my own notation onto the sand,

(where razor shells are sea-quavers playing pitch and toss with time)
and leave behind my song

with this wish, that it too
pulse a memory beyond the reach of the repeating sea.

Tom

Named without ceremony
disposed of with less.

That day skulked round the house and yard oblivious
swaying from head to tail
a ropebridge of bone.

His mistress away at work.

Inside four fully grown men hatching a plan
two with city sensibilities
two with none.

And the Bull Downes
his hospital consultant's gentle prognosis
rubber gloves and a barrel of water
bringing me back to number one Hatch Place
to our dynasty of unwanted cats
— the Fang dynasty —
safariing through the bins of the Eye and Ear by night.

If we'd had the guts we would have taken
those small wet calamities of flesh
from under the old mangle in the lean-to
in a sack to the Grand Canal,
but we let them grow to run wild
over the building sites of future life assurance companies.

Barbershop

You've been there man, to the barbershop,
still trading — anti-fashion like —
under the family name,
oblivious to the trend of hairdressers
for names like: *A Cut Above,
Beyond the Fringe, Hair Unlimited*,
the pole painted in stick of rock colours
on the wall outside.

It's where you go to look yourself in the eye,
to face up to the mirror photograph
as it snaps a moment if not an age,
watch the latest version changed
in pit-stop style by the barber's pale hands
working his scissors to a furious whisper.

Me, I hope to be king
for the length of a dry cut,
but I sit uneasy at the workshop ethic
that turns out class statements
in a crew cut or skinhead,
the shaver as branding iron.

Afterwards I can't help but feel
I've been granted a reprieve
as if from the guillotine's wooden block —
there's a breeze on my neck,
my trophy head's a little tender.
Welcome to my other life.

Letting Go

Letting go of one life
is like a small boy's tumble when tired
a delicate, unstoppable tightrope walker's step into air
that bandy chaplinesque stagger
ambushed by the corner of a table
a stone on a gravel path
the back of a chair.

It's never the thump of a body
spread out on a tiled floor.

Holiday

Something holds them in the house,
four children and four adults
on a mid-term break in February.
By the second day they're calling
the cottages humane tourist traps.

The children play indoors, hide and seek,
musical statues, other children's games.
They keep busy on the raw material of memory,
crayoning kids under a custard sun, a tree in curlers.
The grown-ups make-believe the weather one side,

themselves another, declare the game relievio
mark out the house a den and scatter.
They hide out in the games room
or in the swimming pool and sauna
and sometimes go on cabin-fever

reliever runs to Miltown Malbay or Lahinch
for a glimpse of the world. By this
mind-trickery they survive the week,
the push and shove of the wind,
its ghostly, mischievous grip.

Learning to Cycle

I dropped from the iron railings at the back of the Eye and Ear
where the Victorian sign read *entrance for outdoor patients*
and straddled the crossbar of an over-sized crock
we must have fished from the Iveagh Market
or Charlie Byrnes bric-a-brac shop on Richmond Street.

My mates looked on, half-hearted, listening to the distant
bounce of voices on Leeson Street concrete,
the gear box apnoea of aging double-deckers panting up to the canal.
My own breathing seemed oceanic,
almost too much for my six or seven year old body
as I cast off into the swell of the lane
on the wave of an out-breath.
The pedals turned as if of their own will,
my narrowing eyes-ahead telescoped
a line of lane to a tyre's width
and took me out of myself.

Something unlocked. A dog barked.
My knees pumped me back to the musical ticking
of wheels spinning round, cranked out
like the words to a Dylan or Donovan song
I can still remember when called upon
more than thirty five years on.

The Chauffeur Explains

It's not a dead-end job. It's open ended.
Every day's different. Who knows where
the journey starts or finishes up.
No two trips ever the same. Access all areas.
Tho' alphabetically speaking
journeys are short. From A to B.
That's the gear-shift
of forty years on the go,
I'm telling you.
All day, every day,
the boxer's feet on the pedals,
a light shimmy, no sudden stops.
You should check out the car.
RayBan black. An E 320 series,
parked outside in the taxi-only zone.
Closing the doors is like sealing in a sigh.
And the client? Polished.
I picked her out from the composite crowd in arrivals.
She posed when she heard the snapping of the automatic door.
All these years, I've learnt one thing:
they're just people who long for immortality
but don't know how to keep busy on a rainy day.

Returning

In a tunnel of wind I hear the news
rain, darkness, the ends of the earth,
a fisherwoman.

Always on the return
another one gone.

Gouged out in a glaciated valley
the sea's tongue licking an open grave,
too soon its unexpected rebate.

I take shelter and listen;
hailstones humming a wicked tune,
the snow a crescent on Knocknadobar.

And above, redpolls and siskins
wheeling in the air;
their return to the earth,
your return to the sea.

Sea Currency

They say he's pouring money into the island.
I picture coins tumbling down a chute like gravel or cement
a foundation laid with copper and silver
notes insulating cavity walls and slate roofs
cheques and bank drafts under timber floors
so that when a phlegmy rattle draws me
behind this nineteen-ten Blasket home
and I find shingle piled high
not long hauled up from a stoney beach
glittering like newly-minted coinage
I think of how islanders filtered
the same sea currency through their fingers
to select tokens to draw lots with
so they could divvy-up the day's catch, the seaweed
or the wreckage of a ship washed up on the shore.

Nursing Home

When I grow old and troublesome
I want to live in a place like this
and call it a madhouse
when my son visits once a year.
I will sign a form agreeing to be cared for
by strangers working to a code I don't understand
and happily relate my symptoms to all the doctors and nurses.
I won't mind if I never see the same one twice.

I know I'll never want to leave
so I'll pick my nose and chew my dentures
like the other patients on the ward
and hope my case is kept under continuous review.
And to show how much I appreciate the set-up
I'll ask that my hernia operation be postponed
indefinitely so that all the pretty trainee nurses
get a chance to feel my testicles and be amazed
at how far down my stomach lining has dropped.

I would also happily recommend the coffee dock,
the smoking hut and the vision of health offered
by the straight and narrow of the 9-hole pitch and putt
in the grounds outside to all my friends – if I had any.

It would be churlish to say how sometimes the place
shrinks one's view of the world to a grim end point
so I'll end on a positive note by mentioning
Matron's hardwired smile and say how much
I enjoy the blue light therapy of the television
always on in the common room and my daily stroll
up and down the corridor with the other patients
as we sleep-walk our way to the door marked Exit.

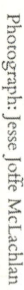

NICHOLAS MCLACHLAN was born in Dublin and lived for many years in lower Leeson Street, Hatch Place and York Street. After a long career as an athlete with Donore Harriers he moved to Kerry to write. His poems have appeared in a variety of journals, anthologies, broadsheets, artist catalogues and festschrifts and he was selected for the Poetry Ireland Introductions series in 2004. His first published short story won the Martin Healy Short Story Award. His stories have been published in *The Irish Times, Force 10* and the *Cork Literary Review*. He has produced and edited two books: *80mph – A Festschrift for Leland Bardwell* and *Ildána*, a bi-lingual book featuring the work of over eighty west Kerry artists and writers. He is a tutor on the creative writing adult education programme in Dingle. For fifteen years he was director of Dingle Writing Courses, an organisation he founded with his partner Abigail Joffe. He lives under Mount Eagle in Ventry, County Kerry. *The Rain Barrel* is his first poetry collection.